# Arthur and the Mystery of the Stolen Bike

Long tail Books

ISBN 979-11-86701-04-1 14740

Longtail Books

For my sister Kim,

and her family, Dave and Miles

# Chapter 1

The Frenskys were eating dinner in their apartment. At least Mr. and Mrs. Frensky and their older daughter, Catherine, were eating dinner. Their younger daughter, Francine, was not eating at all. She was just sitting in her chair with her arms **fold**ed.

"Francine's **sulk**ing," said Catherine.

"I am not," said Francine. "I don't even know what that means."

"It means you're a little, uh, **out of sorts**," said her father, Oliver. "A **bit** upset about not **get**ting **your way**."

"Well, why shouldn't I be?" said Francine.

"I'm sorry, honey," said her mother, Laverne. "But we can't **afford** to get you a new bike right now. Maybe next year . . ."

Francine continued to sulk. "It's not **fair**. I'll just *die* without a bike."

Her father **gasp**ed. "No, say it's not true!" He **drop**ped to one **knee** and **grab**bed Francine's hand. "You mustn't **give up**, honey. Live, I say, *live!*"

He would have continued, but Francine started to **giggle**. Pretty soon he was laughing himself.

"Oh, Dad," said Catherine, "do you really think a **silly trick** like that will work?"

Her father **salute**d her and stood up straight and tall. "Well, it **work**ed **on** *you* when you were Francine's age." He **stroke**d his **chin**. "But perhaps you're right. I don't know what **came over** me. **Besides**, I have an idea."

He got up from the table and held out his hand to Francine. "Come with me," he said.

They went down to the **basement**, where the Frenskys had a **storage compartment**. While her father un**lock**ed it, Francine sat on the **bottom** step. She didn't see the **point** of coming down here. It was dark, there were **cobweb**s, and the air smelled a little funny.

"**Aim** that **flashlight** over this way," said her father.

Francine pointed the light toward the corner.

"That's better." Mr. Frensky **rummage**d around behind some boxes. "Aha! Here it is!"

He moved a box **aside** to **reveal** an old bicycle. Then he **wheel**ed it over to her.

"Drumroll,★ please!"

Francine**'s face fell**. This bike was not only old. It was also ugly. **Bright** purple with **chip**ped

---

★ **drumroll** 드럼을 연속해서 치는 것.

paint, **rust**ed **handlebar**s, and a **glitter**y **burn**t-orange★ banana seat.

"What *is* it?" she asked.

"Your new bike," her father explained. "Well, actually it's an old new bike." He **wipe**d off an **enormous** cobweb between the handlebars.

"Dad, bikes have changed a lot since the Stone Age.✻"

Her father **inspect**ed it. "I don't know about that. They still have two wheels, a seat, and handlebars. And you don't see a banana seat like this every day. **Definite**ly a **collector**'s item."

"But I don't want a collector's item. I want a cross bike❋ with twenty-one **gear**s."

Her father laughed. "All those gears just get **confusing**. Three gears are **plenty**." He

---

★ **burnt-orange** 어둡고 진한 주황색.

✻ **Stone Age** 석기시대. 돌을 이용하여 도구를 만들어 쓰던 시대를 말한다.

❋ **cross bike** 경주용과 산악용을 혼합한 자전거. 속도감을 즐기면서 비포장도로도 달릴 수 있는 것이 특징이다.

**click**ed through them as he **spun** the wheels. "All this needs is a little oil. It's in great shape. When I was your age, I **rode** it to school every day. I know you'll come to **appreciate** it as much as I did."

He **pat**ted the seat happily.

Francine just **sigh**ed. "If you say so," she said.

But she didn't have much hope.

# Chapter 2

"It's not a bicycle," Arthur was saying. "Bicycles can't fly."

"Well, that's true," Buster **admit**ted. They were talking about last night's episode of *The Bionic Bunny Show*. The bunny had a new **vehicle** for **chasing villain**s and **assorted** bad guys.

"I never watch that show," said Muffy, **lock**ing up her bike. "There are much more **educational** and important things to watch."

"Like what?" Buster and Arthur said together.

"The Home Shopping **Channel**, of course. If you don't pay **attention** to that, you can miss some really **fabulous** buying **opportunities**."

Buster **rolled his eyes**. "I'll **take my chances**," he said.

"Take your chances with what?" asked Francine as she **rode** up behind them and got off her bike.

Buster turned to her. "With **skip**ping the Home Shopping—" He stopped talking and **stare**d. "What's that you're riding?"

The others looked, too.

"Whoa!"

"Where are my sunglasses?"

"Ha, ha," said Francine. "This is my new bike."

Buster laughed. "New? In what **century**?"

"Too bad you couldn't get one like mine," said Muffy. She had the **latest** model: twenty-four **gear**s, a graphite★ **alloy frame**, and **radial**

---

★ **graphite** 그라파이트. 탄소 섬유인 카본을 가공해 만든 재료로 가볍고 탄성이 강한 것이 특징이며 스포츠 용품이나 자전거 프레임에 주로 쓰인다.

**brake** pads.★

"I could have had any bike I wanted," said Francine. "But I chose this one."

Muffy **frown**ed. "But Francine . . . why?"

"Um, **tradition**. This bike was my dad's. It's like a family **heirloom**. He was able to do all kinds of **trick**s with it."

"I *guess* that makes it different," Muffy admitted. But she didn't look very **convince**d.

"The biggest trick," Buster **whisper**ed to Arthur, "will be if she can make it look any better."

Later that afternoon, the kids' teacher, Mr. Ratburn, was showing slides to the class.

"The **wheel**," he said, "is thought to have been **invent**ed **approximate**ly five thousand

---

★ **brake pad** 브레이크 패드. 브레이크 디스크를 눌러 마찰을 일으켜서 브레이크 디스크의 회전을 멈추게 하고, 바퀴를 제동하는 부품.

years ago in the Middle East.★"

"By the Sumerians✱ or the Babylonians?❋"
asked the Brain.

"I always get all those *-ians* **mix**ed **up**," **sigh**ed Arthur.

"It is **confusing**," agreed Mr. Ratburn. "In this case I believe it was the Sumerians. Can anyone tell us what these **ancient** people might have done with their new wheel?"

Buster **wave**d his arm wildly.

"Yes, Buster?"

"Built Francine's bicycle."

Everyone laughed—everyone but Francine and Muffy. Even after Mr. Ratburn ordered them to stop, a few kids continued to **snicker**.

---

★ **Middle East** 중동. 일반적으로 아프가니스탄으로부터 서쪽의 서남아시아와 아프리카 북동부의 이집트에 이르는 지역을 가리킨다.

✱ **Sumerian** 수메르인. 수메르 문명은 세계에서 가장 오래된 문명으로 수메르인은 설형문자를 발명하였고 12진법과 60진법을 사용했다.

❋ **Babylonian** 바빌로니아인. 바빌로니아는 기원전 4,000년 경의 수메르인의 도시국가가 기원이 된 고대 왕국을 말한다. 바빌로니아인은 도시국가들을 연합하여 중앙집권제도를 확립하였고, 함무라비 법전의 공포로 제도를 정비했다.

"Stop **pick**ing **on** Francine," Muffy told Buster.

"Yeah!" said Francine.

"It's not her **fault** she has to ride an ugly, old bicycle," Muffy **went on**.

Francine **blink**ed. "Oh?"

Muffy **press**ed her finger in Buster's **chest**. "Just think how *you* would feel," she said.

Buster's face changed in mid-laugh. He looked **embarrass**ed. So did everyone else. They got very quiet.

But none of them felt as embarrassed as Francine did, deep down inside where nobody could see.

# Chapter 3

After school, Francine **rush**ed outside while everyone else was still talking in the **hall**. She was mad and sad at the same time. This new bike was causing nothing but trouble. It was making everyone look at her differently. She wouldn't **mind stand**ing **out** for something special—like throwing a good fastball.★ But being **tease**d and **laugh**ed **at** was no fun. It was no fun at all.

She went straight to the bike **rack**, half hoping

★ **fastball** 속구(速球). 야구에서 투수가 던지는 빠른 직구.

that maybe this was all a bad dream.

But it wasn't a dream. And her bike hadn't changed. It was still sitting there, in all its **disgust**ing purple **glory**.

Why couldn't someone have come along and **stolen** it? she **wonder**ed. They had the whole day.

Well, even if no one had taken the bike, that didn't mean she had to keep looking at it. **Glancing** around, she **notice**d some **bush**es at the **edge** of the school **yard**. She wheeled the bike into them and **rest**ed it behind a **garbage** can.

For a moment, she thought the bike **gave** her **a** sad **look**.

"Don't worry," she **whisper**ed. "I'm not **desert**ing you. Not yet, anyway. I just need some time to think. And it's better to not see you while I'm thinking."

Then she ran back to the front of the school.

Arthur, Muffy, and Buster were waiting for her. They all had their bikes and **backpack**s.

"Where were you?" Muffy asked. "You **disappear**ed from class **awful**ly fast."

Arthur **poke**d Buster in the side. "Buster has something he wants to say to you, don't you, Buster?"

"Um, yes, I do," said Buster. He **clear**ed **his throat**. "Francine, I'm sorry for what I said before. **Insult**ing your bike, I mean."

"And we're sorry we laughed, too," said Arthur. "You know, my father has a **beat-up** frying pan from his early cooking days. It's all black, with a few **dent**s and **scratch**es. I once asked him why he didn't buy a **shiny** new one to use instead. He said there was something **friendly** about the old pan that just made food taste better. I'm sure your bike was like that for your dad."

Francine **nod**ded. She felt a little better.

"Thanks, Arthur," she said. "And you, too, Buster."

Muffy looked along the bike rack. "Where is your bike, anyway?" she asked.

"Oh, um, I'm not using it right at the moment . . . . I just feel like walking."

"We're going down to the Sugar Bowl," said Arthur. "Are you coming?"

Francine wasn't really in the **mood**. Even though she was glad her friends had **apologize**d, she still **felt out of place**. Why did she have to be the one to stand out? She didn't want people to feel sorry for her—even if they *were* nice about it.

"Maybe I'll see you there later," she said.

Arthur **shrug**ged. "Okay."

"Bye," said Muffy and Buster.

They all rode off, leaving Francine with her thoughts.

# Chapter 4

That night Francine sat on the **edge** of her bed, **bouncing** a tennis ball on the floor.

*Bounce. Bounce. Bounce. Bounce.*

With every bounce, Francine wished for another bike. And not just any bike. A bike that would make Arthur and Buster wish they had one, too. A bike even Muffy would **admire**.

Her father **pop**ped in. "What's that noise? Oh, **practicing** your **coordination**, eh?"

"I guess."

"Practice is important. As your baseball

**coach**, I can **vouch** for that. And speaking of coordination, how's the new bike? Seat the right height?"

"The bike is purple," Francine said **dull**y. "Very purple."

Her father **nod**ded. "That was my **favorite** color when I was your age. Purple is the color of **royal**ty, you know. **Dignified**. **Majestic**."

"Really?" said Francine.

"Oh, yes. It was greatly **value**d in **ancient** times."

"You mean like back when they were **invent**ing the **wheel**?"

"**Exact**ly."

Francine **sigh**ed. "**That figures**," she said.

"So naturally it seemed like a great color to pick for a bike."

Mr. Frensky got a funny look on his face. Francine had seen it before. It was his **boyhood-**memories look. A story **was bound to follow**.

"Doesn't it **ride** great? Did you feel how it **handle**s corners? I remember one time we were going to have a **race** through the **neighborhood**. I had never even come close to winning on my old bike. Then I got this one."

Francine stopped bouncing the ball. "What happened?" she asked.

"Well, we all **line**d **up**. And there was this one kid, a big bruiser,★ who was always **brag**ging about how fast his bike was. You know the type. I wanted to **beat** him **in the worst way**."

Francine nodded.

"So the race starts, and I'm **pedal**ing like crazy. And with the banana seat, I can really **lean** hard on the pedals. I'll never forget the look on some of the kids' faces as I passed them."

"So you won?"

---

★ **bruiser** 덩치가 크고 거친 남자.

ELIZA
RAH!

Her father laughed. "Not exactly. The bruiser won—as usual. But at least I was right in the middle. For me that was a big **improve**ment."

"Oh."

Her father looked at her. "Don't look so **disappoint**ed, Francine. I was really happy just to do better."

"It wasn't that. I was **wonder**ing about . . ."

"Yes?"

"Well, you just said how exciting it was for you to get this new bike."

"**Definite**ly. I thought my face was going to **crack** because I was **grin**ning so widely."

"But don't you see? It was *new* for you back then. It's not new for me anymore. If I got a new bike, I could feel the same way you did."

Mr. Frensky sighed. "I wish I could get you a new one, honey. But we don't have the **extra** money right now. And my old bike has a long and **proud history**. I'm **afraid** that's going to have to **satisfy** you for now."

Francine started bouncing the ball again. She **was a long way from** feeling satisfied. A very long way. And from the way her father was talking, she could tell she wasn't going to get much closer anytime soon.

# Chapter 5

The next morning, Francine walked slowly to school. She had hoped that the start of a new day would make her feel better. But even though the sun was shining and the birds were singing, she felt just as bad as she had the day before.

As she turned the corner, **up ahead** she saw the **bush**es where she had hidden the bike. Her view, though, was partly **block**ed by a city **garbage** truck. The garbage **collector**s were out early, emptying the **trash** cans.

"Uh, oh!" she thought.

Just then, one of the men picked up Francine's

bike and threw it into the truck.

Francine started to run.

"Hey! Hey!" she shouted, **waving** her arms. "Come back here! You've got my bike in there!"

But the collectors couldn't hear her over the **roar** of the truck's engine. They **pull**ed **away** before she could get their **attention**.

Francine **came to a stop**. She was **breathing** hard. This was **terrible**! The bike was gone. What was she going to do now? She could only **imagine** what her father would say.

As she entered the school **yard**, Buster and Arthur **zoom**ed up on their bikes. Arthur **brake**d to a stop while Buster circled around them.

"Hey, Francine!" said Buster. "Want to do some wheelies* before school starts?"

"I can't," said Francine. "I don't have my bike."

---

* **wheelie** 자전거나 오토바이를 앞바퀴를 들고 뒷바퀴만으로 타는 것.

A431

"Where is it?" asked Arthur.

"I don't know," she said. Even though she was partly glad to **be rid of** the bike, she didn't feel **comfortable** telling her friends what had happened.

"How can you not know?" asked Buster. He sometimes **lost track of** his **stuff**, too, but nothing as big as a bicycle.

Suddenly Francine had an idea. "My, um, bike was **stolen**," she explained.

"Stolen!" said Arthur. "Are you sure?"

"Of course she's sure," said Buster. "You don't make mistakes about something like that. Right, Francine?"

"Um, yes. I mean, I had it yesterday." She **pause**d. "And now it's gone."

"Gone? What's gone? " said Sue Ellen, who was just arriving with Muffy.

"Someone stole Francine's bike," said Arthur.

"That's terrible," said Sue Ellen.

Muffy looked **confuse**d. "Why would anyone steal that—I mean, your bike?" She asked.

Francine **shrug**ged. "It *was* pretty old . . ."

Muffy **gasp**ed. "Hey, *that* could be the reason! What if it was so old it was an **antique**?" She started waving her arms. "Help! Police!"

"What's going on?" asked the Brain, coming up behind them.

"Francine's bike was stolen," said Buster. "I'll **bet** it was a **gang** of **international** bike **thieves**. They're probably going to sell it on the **black market**."

"No, no," said Francine, who was beginning to think that saying the bike had been stolen wasn't such a good idea after all.

"**Calm down**," said Arthur. "Let's try not to **panic**."

"We should tell Mr. Haney," said the Brain.

"You're right," said Arthur. "Maybe we can still catch whoever stole it. They can't have gotten far."

"No! Wait!" said Francine. She didn't want to **drag** the school **principal** into this. But it was too late. All the other kids were running into the school.

All she could do was follow behind them.

# Chapter 6

Mr. Haney looked hard at Francine from behind his desk.

"Let me **get** this **straight**," he said. "You were hurrying home on your bike yesterday to do your **chore**s."

Francine **nod**ded.

"And those chores would be?"

Francine thought for a moment. "Oh, you know, cleaning my room, helping to make dinner."

"Wow, I'm **impress**ed," the Brain **whisper**ed to Buster. "I never hurry home to do my chores." They were standing behind Francine with Arthur and Muffy.

Mr. Haney **scratch**ed his **chin**. "And you were hurrying, you say?"

"That's right."

*Francine could see herself **riding** along on her bike, **whistling** happily. **All of a sudden** a big truck came up behind her. It was kind of like a garbage truck, but with a big **claw** on the back.*

*The claw **reach**ed down and **grab**bed Francine's bike. She just managed to jump off before the claw **lift**ed the bike up and **drop**ped it into the truck.*

*Then the truck **sped** off, leaving Francine shaking her **fist** at it.*

"I don't **suppose** you got the **license plate** number," said the Brain.

"Sorry," said Francine. "I thought I was lucky just to escape with my life."

Mr. Haney tried to look **concern**ed. "I had no idea such trucks were **roam**ing the streets. Giant claws, you say? I should report this to

someone."

"We need to **put out** an APB!" said Buster.

"APB?" said Muffy.

"All Points **Bulletin**,★" Arthur explained.

Buster nodded. "The **state** police should **blanket** the **highway**s. They should search every **rest** stop."

Listening to Buster, Francine found herself feeling more and more un**comfortable**. "Um, Mr. Haney . . . I know the day hasn't really started yet, but can I go home? I don't feel very well."

"You do look a little **pale**," said Mr. Haney. "We'll have the nurse **check** you **out**. If she agrees, who should I call to come get you?"

Francine thought for a moment. "My mother, I think."

Mr. Haney nodded. "All right, Francine.

---

★ **All Points Bulletin** 전국 지명 수배. 용의자나 요주의 인물을 잡기 위해 미국의 경찰이나 검찰과 같은 법 집행기관에서 발부한다.

Go wait in the nurse's office." He looked at the others. "The rest of you should get to class."

* * *

A little while later, Mrs. Frensky arrived to get Francine. As they were leaving, the other kids watched from the classroom window.

"Did you think there was something **fishy** about Francine's story?" asked Arthur.

"Fishy?" said Sue Ellen. "It sounded to me like Francine **survive**d a **terrible ordeal**."

"Yeah," said Buster. "But **take it from me**, the story didn't **add up**. I mean, does Francine really **expect** us to believe she was hurrying home to do her chores? How **dumb** does she think we are?"

"I don't think Arthur meant that part," said Muffy. "I think he was **refer**ring to the bike-eating truck."

"All right," said Mr. Ratburn, "let's get back to work."

"Hmmm," said the Brain. "Such a truck does seem a little **unlikely**. Is it possible she **invent**ed that part to keep us from finding out who really took her bike?"

"Why would she do that?" asked Muffy. "Shouldn't whoever took it be **punish**ed?"

"Unless . . . ," said Buster. "Unless the **thief** is somebody *we all know*."

The others opened their eyes wide. "You're right," said Arthur. "We hadn't thought of that."

# Chapter 7

That night the Frenskys were sitting in the living room, watching TV.

"Dad," said Francine, "I have something to tell you."

"Uh-huh," said her father. When he was watching TV, it was sometimes hard to **get through** to him.

"It's about my bike," Francine **went on**.

"Your bike," Mr. Frensky repeated.

Francine took a deep **breath**. "It's been **stolen**," she said. "There was this truck with a giant **claw** and I was **knock**ed off and I'm lucky to be alive."

"Uh-huh," said her father.

"**Goodness**," said her mother, who was paying more **attention**. "What a **close call**. That sounds **unbelievable**."

"You're not kidding," said Catherine as she painted her **fingernail**s.

Francine **squirm**ed in her chair.

"Giant claws?" her sister continued. "Were you in some kind of super spy movie?"

"You don't know everything!" said Francine. "And you weren't there."

"That's enough, Catherine," said Mrs. Frensky, "Francine's had a **tough** day. She got sick at school . . ."

"Not very," said Catherine. "It's not like she **threw up** or anything."

"Even so, you're not helping. **Concentrate** on your **nail**s. I think you missed a **spot**. "

"Where?" asked Catherine, **frantic**ally **inspect**ing each finger.

TUCKER

Francine **let out** a deep **sigh**. "So you're not mad, Dad?"

Her father **blink**ed. "Mad? About what?"

"About my bike being stolen."

Mr. Frensky looked like he **was about to** say something, but then he caught a look from his wife.

"I can't say I'm happy, Francine," he said after a moment. "That bike held a lot of memories for me. But it must be hard for you, too, thinking about someone stealing your bike. But don't **give up** hope. Maybe it will find its way back to us somehow."

Catherine **roll**ed **her eyes**. "Dad, it's a bike, not a dog. Anyway, I think someone in this room knows more than she's saying."

Francine got up quickly. "I'm going to bed," she said. "I need **extra rest** if I'm going to get better."

She gave each of her parents a kiss good

night, **stuck out** her **tongue** at her sister, and left the room.

As Francine was **brush**ing her teeth, she looked in the mirror. She saw Catherine coming up the stairs behind her.

"Sticking your tongue out may make you feel better," said Catherine, "but it doesn't change anything. I want to hear more about what happened. Did you go right to the police?"

"I would have," Francine said back. "But . . . but I, ah, hit my head when I fell off my bike and got **amnesia**. By the time my memory came back, it was too late to catch anyone."

"That's from the movie we saw last week," said Catherine. "You'll have to do better than that if you want a new bike."

Francine didn't want to hear any more. She shut the bathroom door **firm**ly.

"Go away!" she ordered.

She finished washing up and went straight

to bed. For a long time she **stare**d at the **ceiling**, **imagining** that at any moment a giant claw would **crash** through and **grab** her. But it never did, and finally she fell asleep.

# Chapter 8

As Francine was walking to school the next morning, Buster and Muffy met her on their bikes.

"We've got news!" said Buster. "Big news!"

"About what?" Francine asked.

"About the **crime** of the **century**!" said Buster.

"What Buster is trying to say," said Muffy, "is that we think we know what happened to your bike."

Francine **frown**ed. "But I already told you what happened. There was this truck, and—"

Muffy held up her hand. "Nice try, Francine,

but you don't **fool** us."

"I don't?"

"Francine, we're your friends. We can tell when you're telling the truth."

"You can?"

Buster **nod**ded. "Of course. That's how we know you **made up** that truck business. And we even know why."

Francine was beginning to feel a little **dizzy**. "You do?"

"It's because you're trying to **protect** someone," said Muffy.

Buster took out a **draw**ing and showed it to Francine.

"The guys who **swipe**d your bike, did one of them look like this?"

"Buster, that looks like Binky."

"We know," Buster said.

"It wasn't Binky," said Francine.

"But it has to be," said Buster. "Who else is

big enough to **steal** a whole bike?"

"**Never mind**," said Francine. "Can't you just forget about it? It's none of your business, anyway."

Muffy looked hurt. "We're only trying to help," she said.

"Well, don't," Francine told her. "Just leave me alone."

She walked away, leaving Muffy and Buster behind her.

"What do you think?" asked Buster.

"I think she's being very brave," said Muffy. "But an **injustice** has been done. And we have to make it right."

A little while later, Muffy was standing in front of a **bunch** of kids. She was **waving** Buster's **poster**.

"I say Binky's behind it," she told the **crowd**. "And we have to make him **confess**."

"How?" asked the Brain.

"We could **threaten** him," said Muffy. "Any **volunteers**?"

Nobody answered. How could they threaten Binky? He was the biggest kid in the class.

"You're such a bunch of babies," Muffy **went on**. She didn't **notice** that Binky was walking up behind her.

"Um, Muffy!" said Arthur.

"Don't **interrupt**. One of my best and truest friends has been **traumatized**," she continued, **sniffing** a little. "This **deed** cannot go un**punish**ed. And if it takes a Crosswire to fight this **terrible** wrong by herself, then **so be it**. It won't be the first time, and it won't be the—"

"Hey!" Binky called out.

Muffy turned.

Binky **glared** at her. "Are you telling everyone I stole Francine's bike?"

"What if I am? Feeling **guilty** about it?"

WANTED

"No. Because I didn't take it."

"Then who did?" Muffy **demand**ed. "Do you have a better idea?"

Binky **shrug**ged and shook his head. "No, I just know it wasn't me."

"Stop it!"

Francine was shouting from the back of the crowd. "Stop **pick**ing **on** Binky. He didn't do anything."

Binky **grunt**ed. "Like I said."

"Then what happened to your bike?" asked Muffy.

"It . . . it got picked up with the **trash** by **accident**," Francine said quietly.

Muffy **drop**ped the poster.

"Francine!" she cried. "Why didn't you tell us?"

Francine didn't know what to say.

"I'm sorry, Binky," said Muffy. "Can you ever forgive me?"

"And me, too," said Buster.

Binky shrugged. "Sure," he said. "I'm a **tough guy**, remember?"

Then he walked away.

Muffy sat down on the ground. "**All of a sudden**, I don't feel very good."

Francine nodded. "**Join the club**," she said.

# Chapter 9

The sun was **set**ting as Francine and her father **start**ed **off** for the **dump**. Francine had wanted to tell her father that the **thieves** had **drop**ped her bike there to **throw** the police **off** their **trail**. However, when she had tried this story out on Catherine, her sister couldn't stop laughing.

"That's so **ridiculous**," Catherine had told her. "Even for you."

In the end Francine had called her father at work and told him the truth.

"Dad, it wasn't thieves," she had told him over the phone. "It was an **accident**."

"I see," her father had replied quietly.

"I guess if you were really being **technical**, you could say it was my **fault**."

"I'm glad to hear you **admit** it."

"You are?" Francine had been surprised. "You mean you knew already? But you didn't say anything?"

"Because I wanted you to say something first."

"Oh."

"And I'm **proud** that you did. Of course, I'd still like you to explain why you did it."

"Because everyone was **making fun of** me. But I didn't try to **throw** the bike **away**. I was just hiding it for a little while. And then when the **garbage** truck picked it up, I thought it might have **solve**d my problem. "

"And did it?"

Francine shook her head. "No. Things only got worse and worse."

"I can understand how you felt. But it's no **excuse** for lying about it."

"I know, Dad. I guess I didn't want to hurt your feelings. I knew how much the bike meant to you. I'm really sorry. What do we do now?"

"We go to the dump," Mr. Frensky had said on the phone.

And now here they were. Mr. Frensky asked the **guard** a question, and he **point**ed them toward the fresh **trash**.

"Now what?" asked Francine.

"We go **hunt**ing," said her father.

"You mean we have to—"

Her father **nod**ded. "**Consider** it part of your **punish**ment, young lady. At least the bike is big enough to **stand out**."

Francine started **poking** through the garbage with a **stick**. There were old pizza boxes and banana **peel**s and broken toys to push **aside**.

The smell was **awful**. Francine tried holding her **breath**, but that didn't work very well. She **settled for** holding her nose and taking as few breaths as possible.

"I think I'm going to **faint**," she said.

"If you do," said her father, "who knows *what* you'll fall in."

"Good point," said Francine. Maybe fainting wasn't such a good idea.

"Aha!" said Mr. Frensky. He **bent** down and pushed aside some **crumple**d papers and cups. "Look, here it is!"

He pulled the bike up and out.

One good thing about an old bike, thought Francine, is that it can sit in the dump **overnight** and not look any worse.

"Did you really **ride** that thing to school every day?" she asked.

Her father smiled. "**Uphill** both ways."

Francine looked at the bike with new **respect**.

PIZZA

"Wow. Hey, maybe we could fix it up."

Her father **shrug**ged. He took out a **rag** and began **wiping** the bike off.

"How about it, Dad? All it really needs is some new paint."

Mr. Frensky looked at Francine. "Well . . ." He **grin**ned **broad**ly. "What are we waiting for?"

# Chapter 10

Outside the Frenskys' apartment, the whole family was standing ready.

"Why do *I* have to be here?" Catherine asked.

"You're part of the family," said her mother. "And this is a family moment."

"I was **afraid** you'd say that," Catherine **mutter**ed.

In front of them, a white bed **sheet** had been **drape**d over the old bike, which Francine and her father had been **work**ing **on** for a week.

"This better be good," said Catherine.

"Ladies and . . . ladies," said Mr. Frensky,

looking around. "We'd like to **present** Francine's new and **improve**d, completely **restore**d . . ."

He pulled off the sheet.

". . . bicycle!"

Francine and her mother **clap**ped.

The new bike was **bright**ly painted. It was still purple, but now it **gleam**ed like a star. And the banana seat had been **rub**bed and **polish**ed, restoring the **luster** to the old vinyl.★

"Beautiful!" said Mrs. Frensky. "Oliver, you and Francine did a wonderful job."

Francine **beam**ed.

"Thank you, thank you," said her father. "I have to **confess** that the finishing **touch**, the **racing stripe**s✳ on the fenders,❋ were Francine's

---

★ **vinyl** 비닐 수지. 아세틸렌을 주원료로 하여 만드는 합성수지로 투명하며 착색이 잘 된다.

✳ **racing stripes** 자동차 경주를 할 때 각 차량을 구별하기 위한 차량 고유의 줄무늬.

❋ **fender** 다른 차량에 먼지를 날리거나 돌이 튀는 것을 막기 위해 바퀴를 덮은 흙받기.

idea."

"Nobody else has anything like them," said Francine. "Not even Muffy."

"I like the color," Catherine **admit**ted. "**In fact**," she added, holding out her hand, "it might look good on my **nail**s."

"Well, Francine," said her father, "**praise** doesn't come any higher than that." He **pause**d. "And now the moment of truth—the **test drive**. Francine, will you do the **honor**s?"

He **bow**ed and stepped **aside**. But Francine held out her helmet.

"You first, Dad."

"Are you sure? I wouldn't want to **deprive** you of your big moment."

Francine smiled. "I'm sure."

Mr. Frensky took Francine's helmet and **strap**ped it on.

"Be careful, honey!" said Mrs. Frensky.

He **wave**d her worries **aside**. "Don't worry,

Wes
APAR

dear. **Riding** a bicycle is like, well, riding a bicycle. You never forget how."

"Maybe so," said Catherine, "but don't let anyone see you, *please*."

"I'll do my best. Just a little **spin** around the **block**. I want to make sure it's **absolute**ly safe."

He **mount**ed the bike and **wobble**d down the **sidewalk**. As he rounded the corner, he stopped to make sure he was out of **sight**. Then he **push**ed **off** fast and **whiz**zed down the street, his face **lit up** with **glee**.

"Do you think he'll be okay?" asked Catherine as her father **disappear**ed from sight.

"Of course," said Francine. If this whole **experience** had taught her anything, it was that she could always **count on** her dad.